MADUL SERIES ❤

Pre-K Attachment and Parental Love

Frank J. Ponzio, Jr.

and

Stephen Madonna, PhD

The People Technology Foundation

Reviews

"Ponzio and Madonna present an insightful view of love as a consideration in Pre-k child development....

As a forensic psychologist, I see the broken lives of patients and their families when secure reciprocal attachment based on unconditional love and emotional self-regulation were not learned early in the child's development......"

—Vincent D. Philpot, Ph.D., Licensed Psychologist

Pre-K Attachment and Parental Love, by Ponzio and Madonna, presents a timely introduction of love in child development.....

Looking forward to their development of a definition of love for a child's formative pre-school years....

—Theresa Oosting, M.Ed., Hillsborough Community College

MADUL SERIES ♥

The following marks are used in this book:

Make A Difference Using Love (MADUL)™

Pre-K Love®, Pre-K ♥®, Pre-K Love Ed®, Pre-K ♥ Ed® are registered Trademarks.

First Edition, 2020
ISBN-13: 9781735038933

This book is based on peer-reviewed research and the best practices in the fields of psychology and early childhood development. However, this book in no way represents an alternative to mental health consultation. Your reliance on information and content obtained by you at or through this publication is solely at your own risk. The authors assume no liability or responsibility for damage or injury to you, other persons, or property arising from any use of any product, information, idea, or instruction contained in the content or services provided to you through this book.

Printed in the United States.

Acknowledgments

A special thanks to Ms. Theresa Oosting, of Hillsborough Community College, Ms. Nancy McIlrath of the University of Florida and Dr. Vince D. Philpot, Licensed Psychologist, for their diligent reviews of previous drafts of this book, their thoughtful comments and feedback, and their support for our project. Thank you to Mr. Knight Berman, Jr., Ms. Kate Campbell, and Mr. Joey Madia who supported the authors in preparing the book for publication.

Dedication

Frank J. Ponzio, Jr.

God, and my parents, Frank Ponzio (Italian sheep herder) and Theresa (née Lombardi). Without them, this endeavor would not have been possible. The concepts of Pre-K ♥ and Pre-K ♥ Ed. developed from my searching for answers to the question, "What could be the reason God wanted me to continue living after a near-death experience?"

Stephen Madonna

This book is dedicated to all the teachers and mentors that I have had the honor to work with throughout my life. For those who pushed me beyond my comfort zone. But most of all for my son, Christian, who taught me so much in raising him.

Synopsis

This book is the next step in an initiative started in our previously published works, *Parenting with Love Ideas* and *Teach Your Child Love: With Pre-K Love and Pre-K Love Ed.* This is our first book in the MADUL™ (Make a Difference Using Love) series.

The book begins by reviewing the topic love, and how it pertains to *Pre-K Love*. From our research, we developed four dimensions of *Pre-K Love*. These include:

1. Attachment and encouraging autonomy (Johnson, 2007)
2. Being able to read the child's nonverbal and verbal cues (Bean & Rolleri, 2005)
3. Compassionate and unconditional love (i.e., selfless love) (Fehr, 2019; Gardiner, 2003; Sol, 2019)
4. Common descriptors and expressions of love (AdjectivesStarting.com, n.d.; All Pro Dad, 2018; Chapman & Campbell, 2005; Griffin Technology, 2011; Johnson, 2007; Thesaurus, 2019)

In the next section, we look at connectedness and encouraging autonomy during infancy, toddlerhood, and the pre-K years (birth through five). The initial focus is on the mother or primary caregiver as a source of love through attachment. As the child grows, that attachment spreads out to other family members, extended family members, and others, with the basis of secure attachment learned through interaction with the mother.

Throughout these chapters, we incorporate other dimensions of love, such as getting to know your child through being able to read nonverbal and verbal cues, compassionate and unconditional love, and common descriptors and expressions of love, such as being responsive, attentive, and caring. We show how responsive, caring parents can foster cognitive and socioemotional development during the formative years where a child is developing emotional self-regulation. We then discuss how responsive parents can help their child to learn to label their emotions and work on strategies to reduce emotional outbursts.

From a parenting perspective, we look at parenting styles that serve to foster the development of secure attachments. In particular, we draw from Baumrind's (1996, 2008) work on parenting styles, along with positive parenting, to show that, when a child experiences an authoritative parenting style in a loving, caring manner, where parents are in tune with their child's nonverbal and verbal emotional cues and are actively interested and involved with their child's life, the child will develop secure attachments. We draw from examples of modeling and positive discipline in developing both cognitive and socioemotional development.

The last section of the book addresses active parenting and community involvement, as well as some issues related to children with special needs.

Objectives

The objectives of this book are:

- To help parents to help their child have a loving relationship in their preschool years;
- To have parents and other interested parties understand the benefits to the child, including:
    - To fill the child's heart with love rather than hate
    - To have a child feel loved rather than feel alienated or unloved; and
    - To assist parents and others in maintaining a loving relationship with the child.
- To provide material that is applicable regardless of whether the child is raised in a two-parent intact family, single-parent family, blended family, with grandparents, or in foster or institutional care.[1]

[1]Adapted from Ponzio and Madonna (2019a, 2019b).

Contents

Section I: Defining Parental Pre-K Love

It is easier to build strong children than to repair broken men. —Fredrick Douglass

In this section, we explore the topic of love in order to develop a working definition of parental pre-K love. We have drawn from philosophical and psychological theories of parental love. We also reviewed common descriptors and expressions of love in an attempt to build a working model for what pre-K love is. Throughout this book, we alternate between male and female pronouns when it pertains to examples. Examples that pertain to boys also pertain to girls and vice versa.

Parental Pre-K Love

Chapter 1: Parental Love

We never know the love of a parent till we become parents ourselves. —Henry Ward Beecher

The *New International Version of the Bible*, Proverbs 22:6 states, "[S]tart children off on the way they should go, and even when they are old they will not turn from it." Children who experience love, and perceive being loved, tend to have more positive outcomes in adolescence and adulthood. They are more successful in school, outside school activities, work, and relationships as adults.

Research by Cousins (2017) from the University of Warwick tells us that it is important to love your child because the perception of being loved contributes to the child's socioemotional development, prepares them for the future, and enables the child to develop self-confidence. Children who feel loved are better able to express love toward others in their personal and social relationships.

But what is pre-K love? How do parents, teacher, siblings, and peers teach it to pre-K children? Research on Ancient Greek philosophers, such as Plato and Aristotle, led us to review eight types of love:

1. *Eros* or erotic love
2. *Philia* or intimate love
3. *Storge* or familial love
4. *Ludus* or playful love

5. *Mania* or obsessive love
6. *Pragma* or enduring love
7. *Philautia* or self-love
8. *Agape* or unconditional love

Our original research led us to focus on *Storge* (familial love) and *Agape* (selfless love) (Ponzio & Madonna, 2019a, 2019b). *Storge* comes closest to a parent–child love relationship. *Agape* involves unconditional love, compassion, and empathy.

Psychological Views of Parental Love

Fehr, in her 2019 chapter entitled "Everyday Conceptions of Love," referred to companionate love as liking and friendship. She goes on to state that it's a form of *Storge* or familial love. Compassionate love, on the other hand, is related to both *Storge* and *Agape* love. It's characterized by quality of time spent together and familiarity, friendship, and maternal love (*Storge*), as well as selfless and altruistic behaviors (*Agape*).

Clark, Hirsch, and Monin (2019), in *Love Conceptualized as Mutual Communal Responsiveness,* link responsiveness to unconditional love. Infants experience love through a parent's ability to understand the verbal and nonverbal needs of the child, and to be caring and responsive.

Trust is also a key feature of love and developing a secure relationship, regardless of the nature of the relationship, but particularly with our conception of parent–child relationships (Clark et al., 2019). We discuss building trust in the next chapter.

Johnson, in her 2007 dissertation entitled *Parental Love: As Defined and Expressed by Parents of Young Children*, suggested a number of behaviors that parents demonstrate to show their love to their children. She includes acceptance, warmth, affection, empathy, and attachment in her description of parental love. Acceptance is in line with *Agape* or unconditional love as discussed above. Warmth can be expressed in our tone of voice and demeanor, whereas affection can be expressed physically in the form of hugs and cuddling. While affection is a part of *Philia* love, *Philia* love is considered to be affectionate friendship between two people of equal standing, and therefore does not apply to a parent–child relationship (Merriam-Webster, 2019).

Gardiner, in a 2003 dissertation entitled *Children's Perception of Parental Love as a Function of Parental Gender and Gender of Child*, suggested parental love involves acceptance but goes on to include a genuine interest in the child's activities, quality time spent together, encouraging new experiences and developing autonomy, as well as expressions of warmth and affection. Bean and Rolleri, in their 2005 book entitled *Parent-Child Connectedness: Voices of African American and Latino Parents and Teens*, suggested that communication and being receptive and empathetic to the child's verbal and nonverbal cues is an important component to parent–child attachment.

Common Descriptors

In the next section we look at a number of common descriptors and characteristics associated with love. Table 1 is a breakdown of our findings pertaining to parental love.

Table 1. Common Descriptors

Descriptors		Source
devoted fond cherished	affectionate caring	AdjectivesStarting.com (n.d.).
caring compassionate friendly	kind motherly fatherly	Merriam-Webster (2019).
affectionate attentive loyal attached appreciative	considerate thoughtful warm valued warm-hearted demonstrative	Thesaurus.com (2019).
spend time with them; stay the course during difficult times	get to know them; celebrate them; show them affection; believe in them	All Pro Dad (2018).

Chapman and Campbell (2005) discussed five expressions of parental love. We have also included several of the common descriptors discussed in the contexts of the "five love languages" or expressions of love.

Love Languages as Expressions of Love

Chapman and Campbell, in their 2005 book entitled *The Five Love Languages of Children,* discussed five love languages or expressions of love that pertain to children. These authors suggested trying all five of these love languages as your child develops. Eventually, you will be able to figure out your child's primary love language. The authors go on to say that by expressing love through all of the five love languages, your child will feel loved and cared for. An important concept in Chapman and Campbell's work is unconditional love. This teaches the child that they are loved and esteemed for who they are as a person, not for what they can do. We found unconditional love tied to compassionate and selfless love, as discussed above.

According to Chapman and Campbell, for a child to experience love, parents must speak to the child's specific love language. Children can respond positively to any of the love languages, but their primary love language is the one that speaks to them the loudest.

The Five Expressions of Love

The first expression of love discussed in their work is *physical touch.* Common descriptors associated with physical touch are affectionate, demonstrative, and giving hugs. As children develop, they constantly need to be reminded that they are loved through physical signs of affection, such as hugs and physical play. Chapman and Campbell suggest that boys may receive fewer hugs than girls due to social conventions. However, boys and girls need just as many hugs. When children are young, putting them in your lap and reading them a story is a sign of physical touch.

Words of affirmation is the second expression of love that Chapman and Campbell discuss. Communicating encouragement and praise as an expression of love involves praise for their efforts and accomplishments, not for who they are. Be sure to encourage your child to develop new skills, particularly social skills. Sometimes it helps to give a verbal prompt (i.e., *scaffolding*), then encourage or praise as you see fit. It is also essential not to tie your praise to something you want them to do because that sets up conditions.

The third expression of love, *quality time*, involves spending time with your child. Chapman and Campbell suggest that this can be in the form of preplanned events or spontaneous time. Children crave attention regardless of their primary love language, so expect to give undivided attention to your child and limit distractions. (e.g., No cell phones).

This approach is in line with compassionate love from both a familial and selfless love perspective: quality time, familiarity, and maternal love, in combination with selfless love.

Think of it as giving your child the gift of "being present." Eye contact is essential. It is also important to be attentive and show a genuine interest in your child. Quality time experiences are also a good time for mutual sharing of thoughts and feelings. As your child gets older, these one-on-one conversations spill over into your child's peer relationships and improve communication skills.

Bedtime storytelling rituals are a good way to introduce quality time to your young child. Planning memorable things, like baking cookies together or going to the zoo, are also great ways to introduce your child to quality time experiences. Remember, it's about doing something special together in an environment where you as a parent are attentive, available, and in the moment. Grocery shopping and running errands does not generally qualify as quality time to a child.

The fourth expression of love, *giving gifts*, is most effective if given with other expressions, such as hugs or words of affirmation. According to Chapman and Campbell, these gifts, along with words of affirmation, can be a very powerful expression of your love for your child and become a meaningful keepsake for your child. With this expression of love, gifts are not given for any specific thing your child does; rather, they are given independent of the child's actions.

This is an expression of unconditional love. The cost of the gift is irrelevant; it's the meaning of the gift, token of appreciation, or gesture that is. A meaningful gift should serve a purpose in a child's life. Too many gifts may dilute the meaning of gift giving. Some examples of gifts may include a special meal, snack, or treat; something personalized for your child; or something meaningful.

The fifth expression of love is *acts of service*. These are little things that you do to make your child's life better. Acts of service can be physically and emotionally demanding; Chapman and Campbell suggest that you take care of yourself first so that you will be able to do for others. In other words, take care of yourself first or you won't be able to take care of anyone else, particularly your child. Acts of service should never be used to manipulate a child, but they can become a powerful model for your child's development of social responsibility. Again, this is considered unconditional love. Be a role model for your child.

As children mature, they come to realize the things that their parents do as acts of service for them and come to realize the pattern in past behavior or gifts of service. Chapman and Campbell believe that these acts demonstrate to a child how to emulate these behaviors for others in their own life. Examples might include helping your child with homework, practicing for sports events, or doing something extra special when your child is sick, such as renting a movie and watching it with him.

Thus far, we have looked at philosophical and psychological views of parental love, as well as common descriptors and expressions of love (i.e., love languages). We draw from this knowledge to develop our own conception of parental love.

According to our previous findings, published in Ponzio and Madonna (2019a, 2019b) and our discussion here, there is very little available research focusing on pre-K love. There is also a need for more input from parents, educators, psychologists, and theologians.

Our View of Parental Pre-K Love

Fehr and Russell (1991), in an article entitled "The Concept of Love Viewed From a Prototype Perspective," suggested that love can be studied as an attitude, an experience, a relationship, or an emotion. They go on to suggest that because of these differing perspectives on parental love, it is difficult to develop an all-encompassing definition of pre-K parental love. Parental love could possibly be better explained by a multidimensional model.

Based on the discussion in this chapter, we have established a list of four separate dimensions. These include:

1. Attachment and encouraging autonomy (Johnson, 2007)
2. Being able to read the child's nonverbal and verbal cues (Bean & Rolleri, 2005)
3. Compassionate and unconditional love (Fehr, 2019; Gardiner, 2003; Sol, 2019)
4. Common descriptors and expressions of love (AdjectivesStarting.com, n.d.; All Pro Dad, 2018; Chapman & Campbell, 2005; Griffin Technology, 2011; Johnson, 2007; Thesaurus, 2019).

Parental Display of Love for a Child: Is There a Difference?

Lamb and Lewis, in a chapter published in 2011 entitled "The Role of Parent-Child Relationships in Child Development," stated that mothers and fathers play with their children differently. Mothers tend to be more soothing, whereas fathers tend to be more active.

Mothers report higher levels of behavior problems than do fathers (Duhig, Renk, Epstein, & Phares, 2000). Johnson (2007) suggested that maternal love is based on acceptance, attachment, warmth, and affection. Children tend to perceive their mothers and fathers differently. Mothers tend to be highly respected, a confidant, and a more permanent fixture in their lives, whereas fathers tend to be more of an authority figure (Meeker, 2017).

Rohner and Veneziano published an article in 2001 entitled "The Importance of Father Love: History and Contemporary Evidence." In their article, they reviewed several studies and found that a father's expression of love includes affection, caring, nurturing, warmth, comfort and supportiveness, and acceptance, consistent with Johnson's findings (see above).

Christiansen and Stueve, in a book chapter published in 2004 entitled "Fathering With Love and Nurturance," suggested that fathers provide compassionate and unconditional love in the form of acceptance and expressing an interest in, and active involvement with, the child.

Involvement in your child's day can mean asking them about their day and really listening to what they say, spending quality time with them during the day, and showing support and encouragement. Encouragement should be for effort, not ability. Encourage your child for trying. The reasoning behind this is that, when your child hits a wall, they are more likely to give up if they think they do not have the ability. Be patient, supportive, and show unconditional love (Zelina, 2017).

Child adjustment is linked to both mother and father parenting skills. Furthermore, mothers and fathers who have similar parenting styles tend to have better child outcomes and fewer behavior problems (Horvath, Lee, & Bax, 2015). Parenting styles are covered later in this book.

Based on the research that we've presented in this section, mothers tend to be more soothing, warm, affectionate, accepting, and develop an attachment to their child (Duhig et al., 2000; Johnson, 2007). Mothers also tend to be highly respected and perceived as a more permanent part of a child's everyday life (Meeker, 2017). Fathers tend to also be caring, warm, and supportive, but are more physically active with their children (Rohner & Veneziano, 2001).

However, these tendencies might not translate to other, nontraditional families, such as single-parent households or "blended" families. Kramer (2019), in *U.S. Has the Single Highest Rate of Children Living in a Single Parent Household*, suggested that, based on research from the Pew Center, almost 25% children under the age of 18 live in a single-parent household, with no other parental support. According to Duffin (2020), published in *Statista,* there are approximately 5.76 million single mother families and 3.23 million single father families in the United States.

In addition to single-family households, there are blended families that consist of two-parent families with children from one or both parents and, in some cases, there are additional children from the current relationship. There are also children being raised in multigenerational households, where there may be grandparents, as well as one or more parent.

In this book, we've tried to develop ideals on pre-K love that can be used by one parent, both parents, grandparents, older siblings, or other interested parties regardless of whether they are male or female, young or old.

In our review of parental pre-K love we found that attachment and encouraging autonomy, being able to read your child's verbal and nonverbal cues, compassionate and unconditional love, and common descriptors and expressions of love, are all associated with pre-K. In the next chapter, we look at attachment and autonomy through building trust and security, while encouraging the child to explore the environment.

Section II: Developing an Attachment

In this section, we look at two interrelated goals of pre-K parenting with love: security and autonomy. We look at how the loving parent provides a secure place, while still allowing the child to grow, develop, explore, and master the environment.

In this section, we take a developmental approach, covering from birth to age five. We discuss how attachments develop, first with the mother or primary caregiver. Then, we show how they develop with others family and extended family members.

Chapter 2: Security, Attachment, and Autonomy

Children are a heritage from the LORD, offspring a reward from him. (Psalm 127:3, *NIV*)

As parents, we all want our children to grow up with the social skills necessary to feel and express love. This chapter looks at our first dimension of parental pre-K love: attachment and encouraging autonomy. We want our children to be able to be free to explore the environment. But we want them to feel safe, too. From a child's perspective, there is nothing stronger than the bond he develops with his mother or primary caregiver. An infant is totally dependent for comfort, support, nourishment, and so on.

In this chapter, we discuss pre-K love in the context of developing an attachment with your child, while still allowing your child to explore the environment, grow, and develop. The two theories that we've drawn from in this chapter are Erik Erikson's theory of psychosocial development and John Bowlby and Mary Ainsworth's attachment theory.

Autonomy and a Secure Environment

In her 2008 book, *The Attachment Connection: Parenting a Secure and Confident Child Using the Science of Attachment Theory,* Newton discussed that when parents are sensitive to the child's needs, and responsive early in life, the child will develop into a secure person. Within a secure environment, babies grow and develop to be free to express their interests and create (autonomy) using the cognitive skills that they have acquired through thinking out solutions on their own. This is at the heart of the relationship between attachment theory and autonomy, allowing the child to explore the environment while still feeling safe to do so. Parents' values, experiences, perceptions, expectations, and culture also have an impact on the child's early developmental experience.

Erikson believed we all go through a series of psychosocial stages in life. He developed eight stages, which cover the human lifespan. For the purposes of this book, we will only discuss the first three stages, as they focus on from birth through age five (i.e., pre-K).

Erikson's First Three Stages

Erikson called the first stage *basic trust versus mistrust.* During this stage, an infant must learn to trust in the world. This is shown in the trust an infant has placed in his primary caregiver. Trust-building is an important first step in the process of socioemotional development.

In an article published in 2017 entitled "A Proposed Model of Psychodynamic Psychotherapy Linked to Erik Erikson's Eight Stages of Psychosocial Development," Knight discussed characteristics of a loving caregiver. If the primary caregiver is attentive and displays kindness, warmth, and caring (all expressions of love) and is receptive to the child's verbal and nonverbal cues and needs, then the child will develop trust or hope in the future.

During this developmental stage, physical contact, such as touch and hugging your child, may reduce fear-induced anxiety and even aid in the development of brain function. In 2017, University of Oxford neuroscience researcher Dempsey-Jones suggested that early sensory stimulation, such as, touch, holding, and hugging, has a positive impact on the child's brain development.

Trust does not come automatically for an infant; it develops through repeated experience and interaction with the primary caregiver. Consistency here is key. Children who experience inconstant or erratic responses from their primary caregiver will not develop trust in others, and the environment can be a scary place. When an infant's needs are not being consistently met, he does not develop a sense of trust and does not feel supported and secure in the environment.

These early experiences in infancy also set the stage for the mother–infant bonding process, which we will discuss shortly. Although Erikson did not assign ages to his stages, trust versus mistrust is generally said to occur in the first 18 or so months of life.

Erikson's second stage is known as *autonomy versus shame and doubt* and is generally thought to cover ages two to three. This period is also known as the "terrible twos." According to Erikson, a child must be able to explore their environment while feeling safe secure and know that his or her mother is nearby, again setting the stage for attachment theory, discussed below.

During this stage a child is beginning to assert her own will. She has a desire to take on adult-like activities (i.e., mimic or imitate), like self-feeding and dressing and starts to internalize boundaries and limits set by parental figures (Berger, 2014).

Erikson's third stage, *initiative versus guilt*, involves taking the initiative to explore the environment, meet new people, and get out in the environment beyond the primary caregiver and nuclear family. With hope and will, children are beginning to develop a sense of purpose. Children will also begin to develop a sense of pride, as they acquire skills and competencies and a sense of self (Berger, 2014).

Attachment Theory

Attachment can be defined as a tie or bond between the child and a parent or other primary caregiver (Newton, 2008). Bernier, Carlson, Deschênes, and Matte-Gagné (2012) suggested that the parent–child relationship is one of the strongest enduring relationships in early childhood.

Knight (2017), drawing from Erikson's psychosocial development theory, described the process that underlies Bowlby and Ainsworth's work in attachment theory: a secure attachment and autonomy. Ainsworth, Blehar, Waters, and Wall, in a 1978 book entitled *Patterns of Attachment*, suggested that security and autonomy are both associated with the development of early parent–child relationships. However, there must be a balance between the two in order for a secure attachment to develop.

A caregiver should be warm, receptive, attentive, and empathetic (i.e., common descriptors of love) on the one hand and encourage autonomy on the other. According to Chapman and Campbell (2005), in their book *The Five Love Languages of Children*, your child should be able to respond to physical touch and comfort.

Communication and attachment are intertwined because communication is the primary source of determining a child's socioemotional state, according to Bowlby's (1988) book, *A Secure Base: Parent-Child Attachment and Healthy Human Development*. Being able to read a child's verbal and nonverbal cues and sensitivity or responsiveness to the infant's needs in a consistent manner has a direct impact on an infant's socioemotional development (Bernier et al., 2012; Fay-Stammbach, Hawes, & Meredith, 2014). This process instills the infant's confidence in his or her ability to self-regulate their emotions.

Children begin to string together events and start to create narrative around age three. By age five, children can string together a narrative that ends in a high point. These narratives are highly influenced by parent–child communication and conversations about past experiences (Kelly, 2015).

O'Connor suggested in a 2002 article entitled "Annotation: The 'Effects' of Parenting Reconsidered: Findings, Challenges, and Applications" that these abilities are associated with one or more of the four theoretical dimensions: scaffolding, stimulation, sensitivity, and responsiveness.

Scaffolding involves parental interaction during exposure to problem-solving strategies that are age appropriate (Bernier et al., 2012; Lewis & Carpendale, 2009). Several researchers have examined parental skills necessary for effective scaffolding. These skills include verbal and nonverbal cues, physical guidance (such as hand over hand), and prompting, elaboration, autonomy and encouragement, modeling, and support (Bernier et al., 2012; Hughes & Ensor, 2009; Matte-Gagné & Bernier, 2011). Scaffolding involves the parenting love skills of reading your child's verbal and nonverbal cues and responding appropriately with prompting, elaborating when necessary, modeling, and encouraging the development of autonomy skills in your child.

Summation

This chapter covered two key areas of parenting with love from a developmental perspective—security and autonomy. In this chapter, we saw how security and autonomy are tied to attachment theory; they are interrelated concepts. The next chapter addresses the four attachment styles and outcomes.

Chapter 3: Attachment Styles

The propensity to make strong emotional bonds to particular individuals [is] a basic component of human nature. —John Bowlby

In this chapter we look closer at the development of attachment styles in the pre-K years. The parent–child attachment bond sets the stage for all other relationships in your child's life (Allen, 2019). Generally, the initial bond is between the infant and the mother, but it develops with any person who serves as an infant's primary caregiver. Attachment theory applies to the important individuals in the child's life, so it's applicable to single-parent families, multigenerational families, and blended families, as well as traditional two-parent families.

Attachment Styles and Learning Outcomes

According to Ainsworth (as cited in Newton, 2008), there are three organized attachment styles and one disorganized style: secure, insecure-ambivalent, insecure-avoidant, and disorganized/disoriented. This section explores these attachment styles.

Secure. Children who develop a secure attachment are easy to soothe, more secure at exploring the immediate environment, more enthusiastic, persistent, and are better at regulating their own emotions and behavior (Newton, 2008; Sroufe, 2005). This is thought to be because the primary caregiver serves as an anchor or secure base from which the child can explore the environment (Belsky, 2010).

Newton, in her 2008 book called *The Attachment Connection: Parenting a Secure and Confident Child Using the Science of Attachment Theory*, suggested a number of positive learning outcomes for children with a secure attachment. Because their needs are being met by the primary caregiver and others, children have a greater capacity to explore their environment. They are able to explore their environment with confidence. They are able to influence others and move around successfully in their environment, because they know their needs are being met and that their parents have provided scaffolding. Remember, scaffolding refers to a bridge from what they can do today with assistance to what they will be able to do on their own later on.

These children have learned reciprocal (i.e., two-way) communication skills, empathy toward others, and the social skills necessary to be respectful and responsive to others (representations of loving others). In addition, these children have developed emotional self-regulation from observing how their parents handle difficult situations because it's been modeled for them through meaningful experiences. Also, they are more likely to have successful future social relationships. Thus, there are a lot of advantages to developing a secure attachment with your child.

Aside from focusing on teaching autonomy in a secure safe environment, the secure attachment develops through knowing and understanding your child's nonverbal cues, responsiveness, quality time and familiarity, as well as selfless and material love dimensions of compassionate and unconditional love discussed in chapter 1.

Insecure-avoidant. Infants with an insecure-avoidant attachment style avoid developing a connection with the primary caregiver (Berger, 2014). They tend to develop hostile coping strategies, such as acting out, blaming others for their problems, and bullying other children (Belsky, 2010; Newton, 2008).

Conduct disorders and depression are more prevalent in these children. Sroufe (2005) suggested that children with an insecure-avoidant attachment style are more likely to isolate themselves from others and less likely to initiate contact with peers and have fewer appropriate social skills.

Parents of children who develop an insecure-avoidant attachment with their primary caregiver tend to be inconsistent in their parenting style and/or rejecting of their child's need for physical contact. These parents tend to withhold physical contact and comforting when the child most needs it, which tends to lead to a breakdown in the child's self-regulation of emotions. This is predominantly due to a lack of positive parent–child experiences.

Children with an insecure-avoidant attachment tend to develop a strategy of pushing away their primary caregiver when distressed. This tendency generalizes to other people as well, such as family members, teachers, and so on. These children do not develop positive coping skills and do not allow others to comfort them. They do not learn to self-soothe and generally tend to have an angry undertone.

The defensive strategies directly impact children's ability to explore the environment. These children do not feel safe and comfortable exploring the environment because they have not developed a secure attachment with their primary caregiver. Also, their socioemotional needs are not being met and they do not learn to self-soothe when upset. Consequently, they do not develop confidence in their own ability to master their environment or autonomy over it. Based on their experience with their primary caregiver or parent, they develop a belief that they will not be successful in life and they have difficulty self-regulating their emotions. They also tend to be untrusting of others and moody.

Insecure (anxious) ambivalent. As babies, insecure, anxious children are overwhelmed and frightened of the environment and tend to cling to their mothers or caregiver (Belsky, 2010). There are two issues here in the development of an insecure-ambivalent attachment: being scared or frightened of the unknown, and lack of physical contact, comfort, and support.

These babies tend to be very distressed and show signs of separation anxiety because the infants' needs for physical contact, comfort, and support are not being met by the primary caregiver. When these children enter preschool, they tend to cling to the teacher and other authority figures to make up for the feeling of security that they don't feel at home. As a result of their early experiences, they tend to be less flexible and more dependent and less assertive and self-reliant than children with secure attachments.

Generally, children with an insecure-anxious attachment do not act out in class or have behavior problems in the classroom. They do seek love from others, such as teachers and administrators (Belsky, 2010; Sroufe, 2005). In adolescence, girls are more prone to seek out love in relationships with people who are incapable of loving them back. Because they did not have positive loving experiences growing up as a child, they fall back on what they know.

Disorganized/disoriented. Children with a disorganized/disoriented attachment style are generally scared, frightened, or confused. They tend to be very cautious and untrusting around others (Berger, 2014). Children with this attachment style grow up in an extreme situation where their parents may have severe psychopathology or substance abuse problems. These problems spill over into the child's immediate environment. These children may be subjected to physical, emotional, or sexual abuse or neglect. Rather than learning to explore their immediate environment with a feeling of being safe (as in the case of the secure attachment), their immediate focus is on survival.

Newton suggests that these children learn to distrust others, avoid relationships, and develop coping strategies to reduce their pain and suffering through distraction, dissociation, acting out, or withdrawing from the situation. Children with disorganized/detached attachment style are more likely to develop a conduct disorder and difficulties with impulse control later in life (Sroufe, 2005). Also, they are more likely to repeat the pattern of disorganized/detached attachment styles with their spouses and children, leading to another generation with of abuse and mental problems.

What Parents Can Do to Help Their Child Develop a More Secure Attachment

As a parent, there are some steps that you can take to help your child develop a more healthy and secure attachment with your child. Yerkovich and Yerkovich, in a 2011 book entitled *How We Love Our Kids: The Five Love Styles of Parenting*, discussed a four-step process that they call "learning to go around the comfort circle" (p. 112).

In their book, they discuss parental awareness. Similar to our second and third dimensions of love (see chapter 1), this requires that a parent be able to read their child's verbal and nonverbal cues while displaying unconditional (e.g., nonjudgmental love and acceptance) and be aware when a situation arises. For example, when a child acts up, there are a number of possible underlying causes. You can use scaffolding, such as verbal prompts, questions, and encouragement to get at how your child is feeling and why.

The second step is referred to as "engage and speak the truth in love" (Yerkovich & Yerkovich, 2011, p. 114). As a responsive, caring parent, your job is to initiate conversation and engage your child. Allow your child to express his feelings and frustrations in a safe and secure environment with unconditional, nonjudgmental love. This allows him to feel safe, and to begin to develop a bond of security with the parent, establishing trust that did not develop earlier during the Erikson's *basic trust verus mistrust* stage of development. This process allows you to develop a more secure attachment with your child when one doesn't already exist. It is also used by parents who already have developed that secure attachment with their child.

The third step is referred to as "explore and find out more; listen and validate." As a parent, your job is to listen to what your child is saying, hear your child, and avoid becoming defensive (Yerkovich & Yerkovich, 2011, p. 114). Mirroring back what the child says is one way to build trust and empathetic understanding. Keep the lines of communication open and use open-ended questions. By modeling this "comfort circle," your child will learn to use it himself when confronted with problems with siblings or peers.

The last and final step in this process is called "resolution brings relief and comfort" to the child (Yerkovich & Yerkovich, 2011, p. 115). Allow your child to share his feelings and put the negative emotions behind him in a safe, secure environment.

It's important for the parent to remember to be sensitive and nonjudgmental (compassionate and selfless love). Yerkovich and Yerkovich have two other suggestions for improving your relationship with your child: make time for him and use that time for meaningful conversations, such as things that interest your child (e.g., an expression of love). Finally, they also warn against becoming reactive in situations and learning to recognize and control your emotional triggers. Respond to the situation, but do not react to it.

Summation

This chapter addressed Bowlby and Ainsworth's attachment styles with a focus on developing a secure attachment and some things that parents can do to facilitate that development.

The next chapters look at how attachment develops during infancy, toddlerhood, and the pre-K years and maintaining a secure attachment with your child. We draw from our other dimensions of pre-love in our examples, such as receptiveness to the child's needs, sensitivity to the child's verbal and nonverbal cues, getting to know your child, and compassionate and selfless love, as well as expressions and other descriptors of love.

Chapter 4: Attachment and the First Year of Life

Infants

At about two months, infants begin to regulate their interior world through contact with the parent or primary caregiver. This is done in a number of ways, such as through eye contact and gazing, facial expressions, making vocalizations, physical contact and comfort, and generally just being sensitive to the baby's needs (Newton, 2008). Mutual gazing, for example, is the foundation for nonverbal communication.

Parents who are more sensitive to a baby's crying are able to reduce the baby's negative emotional arousal through soothing the baby with physical contact, comfort, and soothing sounds. Babies watch parents' facial expressions and begin to mimic the primary caregiver's facial expressions. This is one of the earliest forms of nonverbal mutual communication (Gerhardt, 2015). Babies learn from modeling their primary caregiver's behavior. Moms and dads respond to the infant with smiles, coos, and other soothing sounds, as the infant responds to their facial expression.

By 4 months, many parents begin to understand their baby's different facial expressions. Understanding your baby's nonverbal and verbal cues is one of our dimensions of love. At this point, a bond has developed with the primary caregiver, and the baby begins to take cues from experience with the primary caregiver and begins to self-soothe.

At 6 months, infants are beginning to be more social toward other family members, including grandparents, and are actively exploring the environment. By this time, the infant is starting to understand the meaning of the word "no." This is a real milestone for both the baby and other family members. It also marks the beginning of attachment with other family members. However, it is important to remember that the primary caregiver's face still serves as a model and compass for self-soothing and emotional regulation (Newton, 2008).

Even though your baby has started to let others in, the primary caregiver will still serve as an anchor for some time to come in the baby's socioemotional development. It's important for parents and other family members to understand this and not take it personally if the baby is difficult to soothe or can only be comforted by the primary caregiver.

An interesting phenomenon starts to develop between seven and nine months. The infant might become guarded around unfamiliar people. This is sometimes referred to as stranger anxiety and is a normal part of the developmental process. Your infant recognizes family members through exposure but may not recognize new people in his environment.

Your infant may respond to the new person by staying close, clinging to, or even reaching to be picked up by the parent or primary caregiver (Newton, 2008). Your infant will also look to the primary caregiver to see what her response to this new person is.

Infants begin to show the first signs of intention. An attentive and sensitive parent, older sibling, or relative can soothe the child. This process helps the child develop mastery skills in social situations and over time.

A child with a secure attachment can learn to self-soothe and self-regulate emotions. However, children with other attachment styles, such as insecure-anxious, insecure, avoidant, or disorganized will not be able to develop these self-soothing strategies, because these strategies weren't modeled for them earlier in life in a safe and secure environment.

By 9 months, infants start to develop concepts like predictability and routines. Your baby also develops expectations related to predictability, schedules, and routines. At this age, your baby is able to vocalize and imitate sounds. Infants will start to recognize their own name and understand the meaning of the word "no." They can recognize familiar objects, crawl, or take first steps with guidance, and get into a sitting position without assistance. They are also starting to feed themselves, wave bye-bye, and sit and play by themselves with a favorite toy (CDC, 2018).

Toddlers

At 12 months, your child is either walking or beginning to walk. Toddlers begin to explore the environment and are beginning to develop the concept of autonomy discussed earlier in the book. Also, their first traces of identity begin to form.

The toddler begins to use "social referencing" to determine the safety of the environment. Rather than go to the mother, the toddler will look to the mother or primary caregiver's face for indications that the environment or stranger is safe (Gerhardt, 2015; Newton, 2008). If the toddler sees that the primary caregiver is comfortable, then the toddler will be comfortable in the new situation; however, if your toddler sees any discomfort on the primary caregiver's face, he will react to it negatively by crying.

The 12-month-old is learning new skills, such as communicating through gestures and speech, as in approximations of words (e.g., "mama," "dada"), as well as responding to simple one-step requests, such as "go get your toy" or "bring me the ball." Toddlers are also pushing, spinning, and able to throw a ball; learning to sing and clap hands; copying others' gestures; beginning to use sippy cups and spoons; showing parallel play with other children (i.e., playing side by side with another child, but not necessarily interacting); and, finally, displaying affection in the form of hugs and kisses (CDC, 2019; Newton, 2008).

Brain Development and Attachment

Gerhardt, in her 2015 book entitled *Why Love Matters: How Affection Shapes in a Baby's Brain*, asserts that, between the ages of 6 and 12 months, a baby's prefrontal cortex and orbitofrontal cortex develop synaptic connections that are associated with the formation of mirror neurons. These mirror neurons are associated with the baby's capacity to understand others' emotions and the ability to empathize with others in a sense by feeling what others feel.

At the same time, attachment bonds are being developed. A number of studies have reported that the primary caregiver's sensitivity to the nonverbal and verbal needs of her child between the ages of 6 and 15 months and a quality homelife (attentiveness, responsiveness to the child's needs) are the best predictors of a child's ability to self-regulate emotions in the preschool years (Birmingham, Bub, & Vaughan, 2017).

Summation

In summary, as a primary caregiver, you are learning to communicate with your child nonverbally, through crying and facial expression, physical contact, comfort, and soothing. Babies begin to model the primary caregiver's behaviors. Understanding your infant's nonverbal cues is an important dimension of parental love.

As your baby progresses through this stage of development, at about six months, she will start letting others in, such as other family members. But remember—the primary caregiver is still the primary source of emotional regulation. The infant will still seek out or look to the primary caregiver for comfort and support.

As your baby begins to walk and talk (e.g., 9 to 12 months), she will be more curious about the environment and want to explore. At the same time, your baby will need to feel secure. She will begin to interact with the environment in the form of play behavior. The next chapter looks at the second year of life.

Chapter 5: Attachment at the Second Year (18–24 Months)

The 18-Month-Old

At 18 months, a toddler may still show signs of separation anxiety from the primary caregiver when in public. Children become more aware of being separated from their parents. They are also becoming more aware of internal conflict between becoming more independent and wanting to remain dependent on the primary caregiver (Newton, 2008).

This internal conflict can lead to sudden behavioral outbursts and emotional deregulation. Your child is still learning how to self-soothe. Being patient, calm, and receptive to your child's immediate needs can go a long way toward defusing the situation and soothing your child. Understanding and knowing your child's nonverbal and verbal triggers, as well as compassionate and unconditional love and empathy, will also help to defuse the situation and turn it into a teaching moment.

Children at this age still have not mastered labeling their emotions. Helping children in labeling what they are feeling emotionally will help them to associate a name with the particular emotion. Children at this age often do not have the words to describe more complex emotions, but by helping them describe what they are feeling and putting it into words in a calm and caring environment, a parent – by using scaffolding through modeling, verbal prompts, and encouragement – can help the child to solve the frustration and soothe themselves.

At 18 months, children are going through a period of less reliance on the primary caregiver and more reliance on others, particularly family members. Your child may also begin to show affection to other familiar people. In some ways, this is your child struggling to assert her independence. Sensitivity and understanding will go a long way toward helping your child through this stage of development.

At this age, children are usually speaking in two-word sentences, also known as telegraphic speech. They generally understand more spoken language than they are actually able to speak. Some estimates are that they can speak between 3 and 50 words at 18 months (Belsky, 2010). Some children pick up language faster than others. It is important to check with your pediatrician any time you feel that your child is falling behind or otherwise struggling.

At 18 months, children begin to develop a sense of self and an understanding that they are separate from their parents. They begin to show self-awareness and self-recognition. As they develop emotional self-regulation, there should be fewer incidences displaying anger or fear. But, these incidents are more focused and have a specific target (Berger, 2014). A receptive and empathic parent can help a child relieve his frustration and often defuse the situation. Remember, it takes receptivity and understanding of your child's nonverbal and verbal triggers, as well as compassionate and selfless love. By helping your child put a label to the emotion, in a calm, caring environment, and using scaffolding (e.g., modeling, verbal prompts, and encouragement), you are helping the child to understand the emotion and self-soothe.

Children can also walk, run, jump, stand on one foot, eat with a spoon, and drink from a straw or cup. They begin to self-talk and pretend play, say "no," and point to get attention (CDC, 2018).

The Two-Year-Old (24 Months)

At 2 years, there are a number of things going on in your child's life. According to a book published by Newton in 2008 entitled *The Attachment Connection: Parenting a Secure and Confident Child Using the Science of Attachment Theory*, children are curious about everything going on around them and, at the same time, they are learning to put words to objects, experiences, and emotions. They are also pushing for more autonomy and independence. As they begin to use words, their pronunciation may not be correct, they mimic what they hear, so it would be well advised not to speak "baby talk." Using baby talk will ultimately delay the process of learning to speak.

Even at this age, parents must be sensitive to the child's emotions and emotional outbursts. She is still learning to regulate her emotions. Expressions of love, such as sensitivity, empathy, and good listening skills can be used to soothe the child during these outbursts. Children learn from their senses, what they see, and what they hear and perceive. At this age, parents modeling self-soothing behavior serves as a guide for the child to attempt to soothe another child that is crying (Newton, 2008).

However, according to Piaget, two-year-olds can be very egocentric (as cited in Berger, 2014). They may be adamant about not sharing their toys with other children. An observant parent will notice this.

Setting boundaries with a child at this age can be a daunting task. But, if you as a parent don't address this issue, the child will continue to have outbursts. Parents must set boundaries while keeping in mind that the child's feelings are important as well. Allow your child to express his feelings and frustrations and still feel safe. Remember that by now they should have strong attachments with the primary caregiver, as well as other family members. They may be asserting independence, but they are still holding on to attachments.

If your child comes to believe that her wants and needs are not important to the parent, then you've lost the battle. Remember, children tend to be egocentric at this stage; they often cannot understand another person's feelings or viewpoint. This is another teachable moment in your child's life. By helping your child to understand his own frustration, as well as how other people might feel, in a safe, caring receptive environment as a parent, you are able to use the scaffolding techniques discussed in this book. That will go a long way to defuse the situation and start the process of teaching your child about others' feelings by modeling and being kind and considerate toward others.

Sometimes redirecting a child to another activity will defuse the situation before it escalates, particularly in younger children. Parents must be able to handle these outbursts in a "matter of fact" manner, not showing emotion or appearing to pay much attention to the situation. It takes patience, sensitivity, and unconditional love to do this. Showing emotion or frustration or getting upset will only escalate the situation.

By two years, children are able to show independence – and sometimes defiant – behavior when they feel that their needs are not getting met. They are able to mimic and copy others' behaviors and speech, they may get excited in the presence of other children their age and begin to include others in their play. They can point to and name objects and pictures of objects, such as familiar body parts (e.g., nose, ears, and eyes), as well as dogs, cats, birds, and other familiar animals. They begin to sort things by color, shape, and size and match colors.

They become more interested in daily living skills, such as feeding, dressing, and brushing teeth, and want to do it by themselves. At this point, they are attempting to assert their independence. Allowing them to take on these tasks without assistance will help to develop their sense of autonomy. They are starting to use three- and four-word sentences. They are beginning to run, climb, tiptoe, walk up and down stairs, and throw or kick a ball (CDC, 2018; Newton, 2008).

As we've discussed earlier in this book, security and autonomy (i.e., ability to explore the environment) are the two key features of a secure attachment. This is particularly important during this developmental stage because children now have the ability to walk, thus expanding their abilities to interact with the world around them.

Keep in mind that they are still learning to regulate their emotions, so they may "love you" one minute and "hate you" the next. Naming the emotion for them helps them to put a label on what they are feeling (Newton, 2008). Furthermore, it can help your child to learn to regulate his or her emotions.

As your child seeks to become more independent, give her choices that foster independence. For example, "Judy, do you want to wear your red shirt or your brown shirt today?" Give them two choices and do not give them open-ended choices. Also, the choices should be age appropriate.

Children are very imaginative at this stage. At the same time, they are trying to figure out their environment. Children are now beginning to develop insight and creativity (Thomas, 1996). They are using symbols in pretend play. At this age, parents should encourage this type of pretend play. Let them discover new things for themselves. At first they may make incorrect assumptions, but that is only normal. Be patient and gently guide your child using the scaffolding skills, such as modeling, using verbal prompts, elaborating, and encouraging.

Summation

In this chapter we've discuss cognitive, language, physical, and socioemotional development in the context of developing attachment and autonomy. We've discussed several developmental milestones for children and added suggestions for how to love your child through this stage. It is recommended that if you see that you child is falling behind in development, then contact the child's pediatrician.

Chapter 6: Attachment Ages Three to Five (The Pre-K Years)

The previous two chapters addressed infancy and toddlerhood. This chapter looks at attachment and development in the pre-K years. Developmentally, this group is defined by the ages three through five. Because of developmental differences between ages, most pre-K programs break children up into separate classes for three-, four-, and five-year-old children.

Not all children go to a preschool program; some states have mandatory programs, others voluntary programs, and still others only have private (for-profit) programs. Some children spend a portion of their day in privately-run daycare centers, while others may stay home with their parent or primary caregiver. Check with your state for specific guidelines.

Our discussion of pre-K love here is designed to give insights to parents, teachers, daycare professionals, and persons interested in early child development. Again, the focus is on the child developing autonomy in a secure environment, while also looking at getting to know your child. We also draw on examples of compassionate and selfless love, as well as expressions and descriptors of love.

The Three-Year-Old

We now move forward focusing on cognitive, language, physical, and socioemotional development in three- to five-year-old children. As we move forward, we will continue to address attachment and exploratory behavior.

By the age of three, your child is developing a number of socioemotional skills, such as being able to show affection to others without being prompted to do so. She can separate from mother and father easily and show a wide range of emotions. She can copy other's behavior, take turns when playing games, but may get upset when routines are disrupted (CDC, 2018; Newton, 2008).

With respect to mastering the environment, three-year-old children are able to dress themselves, although sometimes with assistance. They may still need verbal or physical prompts to do so. They are usually able to follow a two- or three-step command, such as touch your nose and then your ears. Children at this age are able to respond to their first name. They can also use words, such as "I," "me," "we," "above," "under," and "you," and can carry on conversation using two to three sentences. A three-year-old can manipulate objects, such as levers and buttons, open a jar, and turn a door handle. They can climb, run, peddle a tricycle, and walk up and down stairs with alternating feet. They can turn pages in a book, as well as build things with blocks (CDC, 2018; Newton, 2008).

Based on a secure attachment and experience with the primary caregiver, children are able to regulate their emotions. Children at that this age are very inquisitive. They may ask a lot of questions as they attempt to make sense out of the things around them. They are able to tell stories. Their language development skills are developing at a very rapid rate at this time. They are also continuing to develop their own sense of self (Newton, 2008).

This is an opportunity to engage your child in conversations and teach your child about the world. Since children are inquisitive, they will ask questions (Newton, 2008). Be present and in the moment to answer their questions (i.e., quality time). Let them know that they can ask you anything; show a genuine interest in whatever they want to talk about. Let them know you will answer their questions, if you have an answer. You are modeling compassionate and selfless love, as well as spending quality time with your child.

Three-year-old children want to help; let them. This teaches them a sense of accomplishment, as well as caring and concern for others, which are also expressions of love. They want to show you that they can do things on their own and for themselves. This is an important step in their ability to develop self-confidence or self-efficacy (i.e., their ability to believe in themselves). To believe that they can do it! Exploring and mastering their environment is part of developing autonomy (see Chapter 2).

Positive experiences build on previous experiences. It's important for parents to encourage, support, and use scaffolding whenever necessary as their child goes through this developmental process.

The Four-Year-Old

Four-year-old children can do a lot of things for themselves. They enjoy doing new things and exploring the environment. They are very creative and enjoy playing make believe – although at times the child may not be able to tell the difference between reality and make believe. Children at this age continue to be talkative, especially about their interests and things that they want to do. This is a good time to take interest in their day-to-day activities and to use storytelling to impart lessons to them. It's not just about reading them stories, but engaging them in discussing the stories, the characters, and the lessons learned.

Children this age are also becoming more socially aware of their immediate environment and would rather engage with other children than self-play. They also become more cooperative with others and begin to understand and use rules (CDC, 2018; Newton, 2008).

As far as cognition and language development, children are starting to learn grammatical rules, reciting poems or songs, and telling jokes. They also are beginning to remember parts of a story. They understand concepts like large and small, light and heavy.

They can name primary colors and shapes and put together a puzzle of 12 to 15 pieces. They are beginning to copy letters and understand the concept of time. They can come up with an ending when read from a storybook (CDC, 2018; Newton, 2008).

As a parent, you can help them to develop these skills through unconditional love, patience, encouragement, and expressing a true interest in your child's daily life (compassionate and selfless love). Furthermore, you can spend quality time with them, you can sit and read with them or tell stories, and you can let them tell you stories. You still may need to use verbal prompts or questions from time to time, but you can help them to continue to develop through scaffolding.

Children can now do puzzles, and they can identify shapes, colors, and objects. Using these newly developing skills, interest in your child, and a little quality time can go a long way toward developing your child's vocabulary and communication skills, as well as strengthening your child's attachment bond. Effort on your part should lead to positive future outcomes for your child.

Physically, your child can hop or stand on one foot for at least two seconds, catch a ball at least some of the time, and pour a drink (CDC, 2018). Encouraging play time will help to develop motor coordination skills.

In summary, by this age, children are more interested in playing with other children, understand rules, are more cooperative, and are very talkative. They are becoming more interested in playing with friends and need less direct support from their parents. They are taking one more step toward autonomy.

Being able to read your child's nonverbal and verbal cues at this stage is still very important. Furthermore, you must display patience and caring and show a real interest in your child's everyday life (through quality time), as well as encourage your child when necessary and praise your child's efforts. And finally, as a parent, you must be able to know when to let go and let your child explore the environment even further and know when to provide a safe haven to come back to (Knight, 2017).

The Five-Year-Old

Five-year-old children want to please or be liked by their friends. They are more likely to agree with game rules as set by elder children, and engage in song, dance, or acting. They show more independence in the absence of an adult figure. They are aware of their gender and know their name and address. They can better tell reality from make believe (CDC, 2018; Newton, 2008).

A five-year-old can speak clearly and tell a simple story of several sentences. They are able to use future tense and count objects up to 10. They can name at least six body parts, print some numbers and letters, and draw some and shapes, stand on one foot for 10 seconds, hop, swing, use a fork and spoon, and use the toilet independently (CDC, 2018; Newton, 2008).

By age five, children are becoming more independent and have a good grasp of language. Providing a stimulating environment with opportunities for your child's growth and enrichment has been linked to cognitive development in a number of studies (Bradley, McKelvey, & Whiteside-Mansell, 2011; Lugo-Gil & Tamis-LeMonda, 2008). Cognitive stimulation occurs through daily interaction and talking to your child, telling stories, sharing experiences, and allowing children to tell you about their interests.

One final note on attachment. Regardless of your child's age, it is very important to be able to read your child's nonverbal and verbal cues. Eanes (2016) suggested a prompt response to your child's cues that she is in distress. Understanding your child's daily routines, such as play time, meals, rest time, and so on is also very helpful in soothing and teaching your child to self-soothe. Finally, as Eanes suggested, when comforting your child, be present in the moment and provide positive attention. That means showing a genuine interest and concern for the child, being present and in the moment (e.g., no phone, texting, or other distractions).

Summation

This chapter covers the development of cognitive, language, physical, and socioemotional skills in the context of attachment behavior in three- to five-year-old children. We also discuss parenting with love. It is important to remember that if you see that your child is falling behind in any area of development, then contact her pediatrician. Later chapters will cover some considerations for children with developmental delays or special needs. The next chapter addresses parenting styles and parenting.

Section III: Parenting

The third section starts with Baumrind's (2008) four parenting styles and developing parenting skills with love. These parenting styles focus on two dimensions: demandingness (i.e., parental expectations) and responsiveness. We then look at the three skills that go into love lessons (Yerkovich & Yerkovich, 2011). These love skills are associated with socioemotional development, particularly emotional self-regulation. Finally, we touch on positive parenting and modeling love through being an example of love to your child.

Chapter 7: Parenting and Parenting Styles

When you look at your life, the greatest happiness is family happiness. —Dr, Joyce Brothers

Parenting Styles

Dana Baumrind developed four parenting styles that ascribe to two dimensions: demandingness and responsiveness. Demandingness is seen as parental expectations for one's child. Parents with a high degree of demandingness set goals that are age-appropriate and realistic for their children and expect results (Streight, 2008). In other words, they set the bar high, but they also expect the child to follow through and complete the task assigned.

Responsiveness, on the other hand, is associated with love support, and understanding on the parents' part, while fostering autonomy or independence in the child (Streight, 2008). Baumrind (2008), in a chapter entitled "Authoritative Parenting for Character and Competence," suggested that responsiveness is a balancing act between the child's need for security and his need for autonomy. In Chapter two, we discussed Erikson's first two stages of basic trust and autonomy, and Ainsworth and colleagues' (1978) focus on feeling secure while exploring the environment (autonomy). There is a common thread in these three theories –.warmth, responsiveness, and security on the one hand and setting goals, expectations, and encouraging autonomy on the other. The next section discusses Baumrind's four parenting styles in the context of developing autonomy in a safe and secure environment for your child.

Permissive Parenting. Permissive parents are sometimes referred to as indulgent parents. These parents tend to be high in responsiveness, but low in demandingness. Communication and nurturing are high, but structure, rules, and age-appropriate expectations are absent. The child grows up in a child-centered environment where the parent just wants to be the child's friend (Baumrind, 2008; Belsky, 2010). This is not a successful parenting strategy. Children grow up with lack of respect for their parents and poor impulse control (self-regulation of emotions). They are used to getting what they want, particularly from their parents, and expect others to respond the same.

Permissive parents are very nurturing and accepting, but they do not make any demands on the child toward maturity. At the same time, they do not feel responsible for guiding their child toward adulthood (Berger, 2014). This leads to immaturity, instability, and lack of emotional self-regulation in these children later on in life (Baumrind, 2008). Children growing up in this environment lack self-control and emotional regulation (Belsky, 2010).

They are prone to outbursts and temper tantrums and generally do not respect their parents. They lack responsibility for their own actions, respect for others, and the ability to self-regulate their emotions, in part because it was not modeled for them during their early developmental period.

Unengaged/Neglectful Parenting. Unengaged parents are physically present, but do not provide either structure or nurturing. They are low in demandingness and low in responsiveness. Generally, unengaged parents are cold, distant, unaware of their child's behaviors or needs, and seem not to care (Berger, 2014). These parents tend to be emotionally distant, detached emotionally, and wrapped up in their own lives. They discourage their children from being dependent on them for anything other than very basic needs, such as shelter, food, and clothing (Baumrind, 2008; Belsky, 2010). They are emotionally unavailable to their children. Children growing up in this type of environment are at risk for abuse (Belsky, 2010). Because of their unmet attachment needs in young childhood, they have difficulty establishing and maintaining relationships with others later on in life.

Children with unengaged/neglecting parents may develop an avoidant attachment or disoriented attachment depending on how much neglect is displayed throughout childhood. These children miss out on having a secure relationship with their parents. These parents do not display any genuine interest in their children's day-to-day life, they haven't had a chance to really get to know their child, and compassionate and selfless love seems to be absent as well.

Authoritarian Parenting. The authoritarian parent is high in demandingness, but low in responsiveness. There are high standards to be met by the child and rules. Misbehavior is strictly punished. These children are rarely permitted to discuss their feelings, emotions, or opinions with their parents. There is little effective communication displayed and parents appear inflexible, distant, and cold (Berger, 2014).

This is not a successful parenting style. Children growing up in this environment are more likely to be depressed and blame themselves for things that are beyond their control (Belsky, 2010). These children tend to have difficulty with relationships and expressing their emotions later in life. Children of parents with an authoritarian parenting style may develop an anxious or avoidant attachment with their parents and others.

Authoritative Parenting. Authoritative parents are both high in demandingness and responsiveness (Baumrind, 2008). Authoritative parents expect mature (age-appropriate) behavior and set high expectations for their children but allow their children to work out their own problems at their own pace. They are more flexible and communicate with their children. They foster independence and individuality through understanding. Parental focus is on fostering high levels of autonomy within a safe and structured home environment. Children are encouraged to reflect on, and challenge differing ideas and play a part in negotiating family rules (Baumrind, 1996).

The authoritative parenting style fosters the development of autonomy in a safe and secure environment, while developing mutual respect and negotiating skills (O'Reilly & Peterson, 2014). Parents display warmth and understanding. Children grow up to be happy, articulate, successful members of society (Belsky, 2010).

The authoritative parenting style is high in warmth and nurturing, moderate to high on discipline and structure, with one caveat… a lot of discussion, moderate on expectations of maturity, and high on communication in both directions (parent/child and child/parent) (Belsky, 2010; Berger, 2014). Children with authoritative parents tend to have secure attachments with their parents and others.

Helping children understand and empathize with those that they have hurt is an expression of parental love. This takes discipline out of the realm of being punitive and creates "teaching moments." By explaining your reasoning, you are showing your child respect and by allowing them to reason alternative ways of expressing their needs. You are teaching them how to regulate their own behavior and emotions (Watson, 2008). As your child begins to understand problems, as a parent you can work with them to find solutions. Over time, they will begin to develop their own solutions (Watson, 2008).

When it comes to parenting styles, the authoritative style is in line with both creating a secure environment, while allowing children to explore their environment, grow, and develop. It's important to recognize that both parents have to be invested in the authoritative style for it to be most successful. However, if only one parent is available, it is still quite effective as a parenting strategy.

What Can Be Done to Break the Cycle?

Parents that recognize their own contributing behaviors (triggers) and parenting styles can work toward a healthier parenting style, such as authoritative parenting. Furthermore, when both parents join together and present a united front and consistency, the overall dynamics of your parent–child relationship can change.

One approach, comfort circles (discussed in Chapter 3) applies as a way to break the cycle, listen to your child in a nonjudgmental way while getting to the root cause of the problem, and providing scaffolding, prompting questions, feedback, encouragement toward a solution, as well as having the child participate in developing the solution (Yerkovich & Yerkodvich, 2011). This approach has an advantage here. By showing an interest in your child, you will be better at reading your child's nonverbal and verbal triggers. You also demonstrate compassionate and selfless love to your child, while navigating the world of autonomy and security.

This approach also fits very well with developing a secure attachment with your child, as well as the degree of warmth and demandingness necessary to usefully use the authoritative parenting style. Remember, you want to provide warmth and comfort (security), while at the same time holding your child to high but obtainable expectations.

Love Lessons

Yerkovich and Yerkovich, in a 2011 book entitled *How We Love Our Kids: The Five Love Styles of Parenting*, suggest that "children develop three essential abilities from good love lessons: (1) the capacity to see oneself clearly, (2) the expertise to deal effectively with a wide range of emotions, and (3) the capacity to repair relationships by dealing with conflict and reaching resolution" (p. 23).

Let's look at these three abilities. So then, what is self-awareness? It's a skill that is taught to a child when the parent is open in the moment, focuses all their attention on the child, actively listens to the child, and "loves the heart" of the child. This kind of love is selfless and unconditional love. It's nonjudgmental. Attentiveness, feeling valued, caring, spending time, getting to know and believing in the child are all at work here (All Pro Dad, 2018; Griffin Technology, 2011; Thesaurus, 2019).

The ability to deal with emotions involves the ability to deal with stress. For a child, too much stress can be traumatic. On the other hand, parents cannot fix children's problems for them. Parents that try to fix all their children's problems tend to do their children a disservice.

As we discussed in Chapter two, children need to be able to solve their own problems and learn to self-regulate their behavior and emotions. One of the goals of pre-K love is to help them to become more autonomous in a responsive, secure, and caring environment.

According to Yerkovich and Yerkovich, parents should help prepare children to be able to feel the stress and deal with it. Parents should be responsive, attentive, supportive, use scaffolding procedures to get children to express the shame, grief, doubt, and fears that they may at times feel, in a safe and supportive environment. Affection, nurturing, and active listening skills (compassionate love) support healthy development in the child.

The third essential ability that Yerkovich and Yerkovich discuss is resolving conflicts. Teaching mutual respect and tolerance are key features of the successful parent. As a parent, understanding and celebrating individual and cultural differences will prepare your child for a culturally diverse and global society. Compassion, consideration, and appreciation are descriptors that come to mind here, as well as patience and communication skills (compassionate and selfless love).

Eanes, in her 2016 book entitled *Positive Parenting: An Essential Guide*, suggests a three-step process for teaching positive discipline that also involves problem solving. She goes on to state that a child's behavior in a given situation reflects an underlying emotion, or what is going on beneath the surface. The behavior itself doesn't always give accurate cues as to what's going on below the surface, particularly when your child is younger, and may not have the words to express what they are feeling. You can assess your child's needs through responsiveness, understanding your child's nonverbal and verbal cues, triggers, and so on (i.e., compassionate love). The behavior itself can be disruptive, but it's important to find out what is the underlying cause.

The next step is to calmly discuss the matter with your child. Keep in mind that younger children may not have developed the words to adequately express what they are feeling, so you can assist by helping your child to describe the emotion and help them to label it.

The last step is to help them to problem solve and come up with a solution. Using scaffolding (e.g., prompting questions,, such as, "What caused you to get upset?" and, "What can you do next time to deal with these feelings?") are often effective ways to get at the root cause in a calm manner, while teaching your child to focus on the solution.

Positive Parenting

According to Eanes (2016), there are five basic principles of positive parenting. As we discussed earlier in this book, infant–parent or caregiver attachment is an elementary part of relationship building. Eanes suggested that it is the standard for developing all other relationships.

Respect is the second basic core principle in her model. Parents who are nurturing and loving show their children the same respect that they would show others. They lead by example! They model appropriate ways of dealing with stress and frustration.

In this vein, parents should be proactive, not reactive. Responsiveness to your child's moods and emotions plays into your child's successful socioemotional development. Proactive parents get out in front of potential problems before they become serious problems. Proactive parents also respond to their children's needs rather than reacting to them (Eanes, 2016).

Finally, Eanes suggested that positive parenting involves empathetic leadership. She suggested that it is important to understand our children's needs, while still holding on to legitimate boundaries and expectations. Children's behavior is not shaped by punishment and reprimand; it is shaped by example, encouragement, support, and understanding in a safe and secure environment. The next section discusses modeling behavior and leading by example.

Modeling Behavior as a Means of Parenting With Love

Modeling behavior implies leading by example. One goal of parents should be to teach their children good moral character and values (Lickona, 2008). Leading children involves treating them with kindness, caring, thoughtfulness, love, and respect.

Modeling behavior is one mechanism for transmitting moral values to our children. By modeling how one should treat others, we are teaching these values to our children. How we treat each other in the presence of the child will determine how our child treats others. If we speak negativity, our children will notice it and mimic that behavior.

Drawing from Bandura's early work on modeling, Morris, Silk, Steinberg, Myers, and Robinson (2007) suggested that children pick up on parents' emotional profiles, which teaches them expectations of acceptable and unacceptable behavior within the family context. It's important for every child to have a role model, someone to which they can look up (Becker, 2019).

Children also connect interactions and outcomes to determine if the behavior is acceptable. Lickona (2008) suggested that two-way communication and good moral reasoning are an important part of the process of teaching children character and moral values. He draws from the following scripture: "Love is patient, love is kind. It does not envy, it does not boast, it is not proud. It is not rude, it is not self-seeking" (1 Corinthians 13:4 - 5, NIV). In this definition, we see unconditional love.

Summation

This chapter looked at parenting styles (permissive indulgent, unengaged neglectful, authoritarian, and authoritative), as well as developing abilities from love lessons, positive discipline, positive parenting, and being an example to your child (modeling). The next section looks at active parenting, getting involved in your child's development, community involvement, and early intervention programs.

SECTION IV: Community Involvement And Early Intervention

This last section is also devoted to parental involvement in the child's immediate and extended environment and community involvement. The final chapter involves special considerations for parents with children with special needs. The chapter is followed by a Pre-K Love Cheat Sheet and information on national organizations and their resources.

Chapter 8: Active Parenting and Community Involvement

In this chapter, we establish a link between active parenting in the home and community, as well as community involvement. Recent studies indicate that early and active parental involvement has a positive impact on your child's later learning and development (Galindo & Sheldon, 2012; Sheridan, Knoche, Edwards, Bovaird, & Kupzyk, 2010). However, research also shows that the experience and activity must be meaningful to the child (Zhang, 2015).

Epstein, in a 2010 article entitled "School/Family/Community Partnerships: Caring for the Children We Share," suggested that parental involvement in both home life and the outside learning environment, such as early intervention programs, Head Start, and church-related learning activities, is beneficial to both the child and the parent.

Community-based activities support children's language and communication development, as well as social skills development. Furthermore, when parents and their children participate in these types of programs, it fosters the development of a secure parent–child attachment. (For more on secure attachment, see Chapter three.)

Active parenting involves nurturing and giving guidance (scaffolding), as well as providing a supportive environment for the child to explore (autonomy). Often times, effective communication involves using outside resources and programs. Volunteering allows parents to actively participate in programs outside the home in which your child may be involved.

Volunteering involves setting aside regularly scheduled blocks of time, setting goals, and finding ways to measure success, which is in line with getting to know your child and spending quality time with her (Gardiner, 2003). Decision-making involves having an active voice in what your child is exposed to both inside and outside the home environment. Ultimately, it is your decision what activities in which you allow your child to participate. Collaborating with community involves finding and working with outside community sources and resources to strengthen family practices, as well as child learning and development (Epstein, 2010).

Community Involvement: Education and Intervention

According to Johns, in a 2010 article entitled "Early Childhood Service Development and Intersectoral Collaboration in Rural Australia," one of the cornerstones of early childhood development is family and community, including supportive parents, a safe home environment, and collaborative community involvement. So, home and community life go hand-in-hand in supporting child development.

In recent years, a number of researchers have advocated early intervention programs for children who are at risk of lagging behind (e.g., Heckman, 2006; Shonkoff & Levitt, 2010). Increasing the availability of parent- and teacher-mediated programs provides opportunities for children from low socioeconomic backgrounds to develop social and educational skills (Campbell et al., 2008; Wass, 2015).

Several studies on early intervention programs focusing on cognitive and socioemotional development have been shown to be a good and short- and long-term investment (Fox & Rutter, 2010; Heckman, 2006). Heckman, Stixrud, and Urzua (2006) suggested that early intervention, child enrichment, and frequent home visits have been shown to improve motivation and noncognitive skills in pre-K children.

Bradley and colleagues (2011) suggested that not all programs provide the same long-term benefit. McCartney, Dearing, Taylor, and Bub (2007) found that the quality of care is the real issue. They reported improvement in cognitive development in children of low-income parents only when parents were actively involved.

Wachs (2000) suggested that the focus should be on matching resources to the child's specific needs. Solheim, Wichstrøm, Belsky, and Berg-Neilson, in a 2013 article entitled "Do Time in Childcare and Peer Group Exposure Predict Poor Socioemotional Adjustment in Norway?" suggested parents should look at three criteria when evaluating preschool childcare programs: (a) the quality of the program; (b) the number of hours per week the child will attend the program; and (c) the type of care that is provided (e.g., cognitive stimulation). Understanding typical and atypical early childhood development is important in developing remedial programs (Guerra, Graham, & Tolan, 2011).

Benefits of Early Childhood Education

Head Start programs have been around since 1965 (USDHHS, 2010). Head Start is a government-funded program that was originally developed to provide early education services to economically disadvantaged three- and four-year-old children that are based on a "whole child" model: medical/dental, nutrition, mental health, and education (Gormley, Phillips, Adelstein, & Shaw, 2010; USDHHS, 2010).

According to Sanchez, in a 2015 TEDx Talk entitled "The 'Head Start' Early Childhood Education Gave Me," Head Start programs are an active means of child socialization with a focus on language development and verbal achievement. Sanchez goes on to say that, in students that participate in Head Start, there are fewer behavior problems and higher high school graduation rates.

The *Head Start Impact Study* is a longitudinal study that has been collecting data on Head Start programs for more than 40 years. This study compares three- and four-year-old Head Start students with a control group (i.e., students that received no preschool training). Findings indicate that three-year-olds were found to have better vocabulary and math scores by the end of the fourth year than the control group (USDHHS, 2010). In the socioemotional domain, students showed improvement in social skills and a decline in hyperactive behavior and behavior problems.

Since the 1990s, there has been more focus on school-based pre-K programs and a number of other programs have developed that are more inclusive (Gormley et al., 2010). Both school-based pre-K programs and Head Start focus on cognitive and socioemotional development.

In a study comparing a state-funded Head Start program with a state-funded pre-K program, it was found both programs impacted cognitive development, but the pre-K program was more effective in letter and word identification and spelling (Gormley et al., 2010). Differences between the two groups were also reported in socioemotional development. Pre-K students were also reported to be more attentive and more assertive in class. The final measure looked at health issues. Here, the results are in the reverse: children attending the Head Start program were rated as healthier by their parents than their pre-K peers (Gormley et al., 2010).

In summary, there are benefits for both parents and children when they participate in community-based activities and early intervention programs, such as Head Start. For the child, both cognitive and social domains appear to develop at a faster rate than when parents are not actively involved. For parents, this participation in community-based programs strengthens parent–child attachments and allows parents to model love through getting to know the child better through active involvement in the child's day-to-day activities (quality time) and other expressions of love, such as acts of service (Chapman & Campbell, 2005).

Mental Health

Early childhood mental health consultation (ECMHC) is an intervention that is based on collaboration between parents, school and childcare officials, and mental health practitioners (Green, Masch, Kothari, Busse, & Brennan, 2012). ECMHC involves using problem-solving strategies and experiential learning to build socioemotional learning competencies in at-risk children.

A number of studies indicate that this approach reduces child outbursts and other challenging behaviors, as well as improves teacher skills and reduces teacher stress in the classroom (Green, Everhart, Gordon, & Gettman, 2006; Raver et al., 2009). This perspective focuses attention on relationship building (Green et al., 2012).

Both parents and teachers play a significant role in early childhood development. From an early age, children learn values, attitudes, and likes and dislikes that are nurtured in part at home.

Thus, as stated in the previous chapter, children learn through observing their parents, peers, teachers, and so on. During this time, children are developing cognitive, language, and socioemotional self-efficacy skills. Children are also exposed to lessons in morality and love. They learn forgiveness.

Teachers, along with parents, play an important role in socializing children. As children begin to develop reasoning and language skills they become adept at picking up tone, intonation, and rhythm in speech (Haider & Ali, 2013). Personality characteristics and patterns are also developing at this time (Haider & Ali, 2013).

Early childhood education provides a forum for learning socialization, cooperation, and teamwork skills in a safe environment, where children are free to explore the environment and learn simultaneously (Palmer, 2016). These skills develop through interaction with parents and teachers and are fostered by scaffolding with physical guidance and prompting, modeling with encouragement and support (Bernier et al., 2012; Hughes & Ensor, 2009; Matte-Gagné & Bernier, 2011). This is very much in line with how children learn in their home environment. In line with socialization, children develop values and respect for others (citizenship) in a culturally diverse classroom (Palmer, 2016). Responsive, attentive, caring parents can foster these ideas in the home environment as well, teaching love though expressing love and modeling what love is for their children. Teachers also have the opportunity to model expressions of love while modeling respect, dignity, and moral behavior.

Summation

Early childhood education sets the groundwork for later cognitive and socioemotional development, which has been shown to positively impact both the individual and the larger economic community (Fink et al., 2015; Heckman, 2006; McCoy et al., 2017; Nores & Barnett, 2010; Peet et al., 2015; Shonkoff, 2010).

Early childhood education and intervention programs provide the support that parents often need in helping their child grow and develop into a productive member of society. The next chapter looks at special considerations in parenting children with special needs.

Chapter 9: Special Consideration for Children With Special Needs

Norris and Rodwell (2017), in their book entitled *Parenting With Theraplay*, suggested that when a child does not develop a particular developmental milestone or milestones during the specified developmental period, then it is important that pediatricians and other professionals evaluate the child and refer him for testing or other specialized services, when necessary. These areas could be communication skills, behavior, learning, movement, sensory processing, and/or physical development (Delahooke, 2017).

Part C of the Individuals with Disabilities Education Act (Department of Education, 2004) addresses early intervention services for children under the age of three. Services are mandated for children with disabilities. Communication, behavior, learning, movement, sensory processing, and physical development are among the reasons that a child may be referred for early intervention (Delahooke, 2017). Parental involvement in the process is vital for your child's success.

Being able to read your child's emotional (nonverbal responses) and soothing the infant will support the development of attachment. Interpreting and supporting your child's need to feel safe is a vital part of developing an attachment with your child (Norris & Rodwell, 2017).

With children who have developmental delays, Norris and Rodwell suggest starting where the child is in the developmental process and going forward. They have developed an approach that focuses on: (a) developing an emotional connection with your child; (b) understanding attachment styles; and (c) supporting your child's ability to self-regulate. These processes have been discussed individually and collectively throughout this book.

Children with attention deficit disorder have unique challenges that may preclude some more standard approaches to developing a loving, secure attachment with the child. The next section looks at some of these challenges.

Attention Deficit Hyperactivity Disorder (ADHD)

Children with ADHD usually display symptoms of inattention and/or impulsivity. Inattention can be seen as a lack of attention to detail, forgetting and losing things, difficulty concentrating on an activity or task, not completing assignments or tasks, and/or difficulty organizing tasks or objects (APA, 2013).

Impulsivity can be seen in a variety of behaviors, such as blurting out answers, difficulty waiting patiently, and interrupting others. Hyperactivity is related to excessive motor activity, such as being fidgety (APA, 2013).

Several of the issues related to inattention can really put a strain on parents with a child who has been diagnosed with ADHD. Attention to detail, forgetting, and concentration issues are all associated with this disorder. It's very important for parents to remember that these are issues related to the child's physiological maturation, and not moral character or laziness. Responsive, attentive parents can provide structure and specificity in their child's everyday duties. For example, asking a child to clean his room is too broad and often too vague to get the response you want to get from your child. As a parent you have to be specific, starting with one particularly thing you want the child to do. Provide structure and encouragement (scaffolding) in the form of verbal or physical prompts and modeling. When you get the response that you are looking for, use expressions of love, such as hugs (physical contact), praise (words of affirmation), and from time to time, a reward. It takes patience and responsiveness. Impulsivity requires patience, as well as compassionate and unconditional love. Use cues, prompts, reminders, and redirection when the child is hyper-responsive, such as counting to three before you respond.

Autism Spectrum Disorders (ASD)

Children with ASD may experience a number of developmental delays in language development and communication, socioemotional development, and developing relationships (APA, 2013). In addition, they may have stereotyped behaviors, such as hand flapping or repetitive spinning of objects. They may express echolalia, which is repetition of words or phrases "out of context." They may also be hypersensitive to environmental stimulation (APA, 2013).

Like children with ADHD, parents who are patient, responsive, empathetic, and caring are more successful with their child. Knowing your child's nonverbal and verbal triggers, love languages, compassionate and selfless love, and scaffolding are all techniques that parents can use to show that they love their child, as well as model what love is to the child.

Parental Stress and Support Systems

Mothers and fathers of children with ASD may experience extreme stress (Delahooke, 2017; Lickenbrock, Ekas, & Whitman, 2011). Parents may not have the coping skills to deal with it. Eanes (2016) suggested a self-work exercise for parents that allows them to get right with themselves before dealing with their child. She suggests that we cannot change our past, but we can change how we perceive our past experiences.

Eanes developed a six-step process for reducing stress that involves reviewing one's past, expressing gratitude where it is due, taking note of blame, describing the future if you stay stuck, planning the future you want, and making it happen. She goes on to suggest that parents have to build discipline in their own lives and learn to recognize their triggers.

Parents' perceptions of their children influence outcomes, particularly with autistic children (Lickenbrock et al., 2011). The child's problems do not occur in a vacuum; parents need support as well. When parents can do this successfully, they are ready to deal with their child's challenges. Realistic hope is a great coping strategy for parents to have (Delahooke, 2017).

Because children with ASD may be hypersensitive to environmental stimuli, they may not respond positively to touch, cuddling, and soothing the same way that other children respond. An occupational therapist can test for sensory processing deficits and be able to give you more guidance on your child's difficulties with touch (Norris & Rodwell, 2017).

It is really important to know your child and understand her needs. Therefore, other expressions of love might work better for your child. Compassionate and selfless love, empathy, responsiveness, and encouragement can go a long way toward helping your child. Quality time, such as bedtime rituals, may work better for your child than physical touch. As a parent, you may also focus on activities that foster nurturing as an expression of love (Norris & Rodwell, 2017).

The more you know about your child's verbal and nonverbal cues and triggers the easier it will be for you to express your love for your child. Looking at expressions that do not involve physical touch is a good place to start in working with your child.

Summation

This chapter addressed a few special cases where more traditional methods of expression of your love for your child might not be effective. We also touched on parental stress that goes along with these disorders. We addressed some alternatives to traditional ways to develop a secure attachment with the child. When in doubt, do not hesitate to contact your child's physician or therapist.

Pre-K Love Cheat Sheet

As much of the focus of this book was on pre-K love, we'd liked to give the readers a little takeaway. We've developed a short cheat sheet that parents, teachers, and trainers and others can use to describe pre-K love.

Pre-K Love

- Parents, teachers, and others show a child love by modeling it through their behavior (Lickona, 2008). Consistency is very important. Be a model of love!
- Expressions of love, such as being responsive to the child's needs, being kind, caring, and patient, all go back to modeling love.
- Chapman and Campbell (2005) described five love languages or expressions of love: physical touch, words of affirmation, quality time, gifts, and acts of service. It's important that parents use all five until you determine your child's primary love language. Even then, it's still important to use all five love languages,
- Show an interest in your child's everyday activities and be supportive, spending quality time with your child (compassionate and selfless love).
- Teachers can also show expressions of love, through kindness, patience, and responsiveness to the child's needs. It's important that teachers also get to know their students, their nonverbal and verbal cues and triggers, and that every child feel included.

National Organizations

For more information and resources for helping children with neurodevelopmental disorders, please see the following organizations.

American Association on Intellectual and Developmental Disabilities
Mission: "AAIDD promotes progressive policies, sound research, effective practices, and universal human rights for people with intellectual and developmental disabilities."
https://aaidd.org/

Attention Deficit Disorder Association
Mission: "The Attention Deficit Disorder Association provides information, resources and networking opportunities to help adults with Attention Deficit Hyperactivity Disorder lead better lives."
https://add.org/

Autism Speaks
Mission: "Autism Speaks is dedicated to promoting solutions, across the spectrum and throughout the life span, for the needs of individuals with autism and their families through advocacy and support; increasing understanding and acceptance of people with autism spectrum disorder; and advancing research into causes and better interventions for autism spectrum disorder and related conditions."
https://www.autismspeaks.org/

Autism Spectrum Disorder Foundation
Mission: "The goal of ASDF is to support children with an autism spectrum disorder by providing information, education and financial assistance to their families and relevant community service organizations."
https://myasdf.org/about-asdf/

Childcare Aware of America
Mission: "Supports children's growth, development, and educational advancement and creates positive economic impact for families and communities."
https://usa.childcareaware.org/

Children and Adults with Attention Deficit Disorder
Mission: "We believe in improving the lives of people affected by ADHD."
https://chadd.org/

National Association for Family Child Care
Mission: "NAFCC provides technical assistance to family childcare associations by promoting leadership development and by promoting quality and professionalism through the organization's accreditation process for family childcare providers."
https://www.nafcc.org/

National Association of Education for Young Children
Mission: "NAEYC is dedicated to improving the well-being of all young children, with particular focus on the quality of educational and developmental services for all children from birth through age 8."
https://www.naeyc.org/

National Autism Association
Mission: "The mission of the National Autism Association is to respond to the most urgent needs of the autism community, providing real help and hope so that all affected can reach their full potential."
https://nationalautismassociation.org/

National Education Association
Mission: "NEA is committed to advancing the cause of public education. NEA's 3 million members work at every level of education—from pre-school to university graduate programs."
http://www.nea.org/home/18163.htm

National Head Start Association
Mission: "The Association provides support for the Head Start community by advocating for policies to strengthen Head Start services; providing training and professional development to Head Start staff; and developing and disseminating research, information, and resources that enrich Head Start program delivery."
https://www.nhsa.org/

National Institute of Mental Health
Mission: "The mission of the National Institute of Mental Health (NIMH) is to transform the understanding and treatment of mental illnesses through basic and clinical research, paving the way for prevention, recovery, and cure."
https://www.nih.gov/about-nih/what-we-do/nih-almanac/national-institute-mental-health-nimh

About: "NIMH is the lead federal agency for research on mental disorders. NIMH is one of the 27 Institutes and Centers that make up the National Institutes of Health (NIH), the largest biomedical research agency in the world."
https://www.nimh.nih.gov/index.shtml

References

AdjectivesStarting.com. (n.d.). Retrieved from http://adjectivesstarting.com/positive-adjectives/

Ainsworth, M. D. S., Blehar, M., Waters, E., & Wall, S. (1978). *Patterns of attachment*. Hillsdale, NJ: Erlbaum.

All Pro Dad. (2018). Retrieved from https://www.allprodad.com/10-ways-to-show-your-kids-you-love-them/.

Allen, D. (2019, August 27). Attachment styles, what they are and why they matter. Retrieved from https://www.therapyroute.com/article/attachment-styles-what-they-are-and-why-they-matter-by-d-allen

American Psychiatric Association (APA). (2013). *Diagnostic and statistical manual of mental disorders* (5th ed.). Washington, DC: Author.

Baumrind, D. (1996). The discipline controversy revisited. *Family Relations, 45*, 405–414.

Baumrind, D. (2008). Authoritative parenting for character and competence. In D. Streight (Ed.), *Parenting for character, five experts, five practices* (pp. 17–30). Portland, OR: Council for Spiritual and Ethical Education.

Bean, S., & Rolleri, L. (2005). *Parent-child connectedness: Voices of African American and Latino parents and teens*. Santa Cruz, CA: ETR Associates.

Becker, N. (2019). *Positive parenting.* Amazon Digital Services.

Belsky, J. (2010). *Experiencing the lifespan* (2nd

ed.). New York, NY: Worth Publishing.

Berger, K. S. (2014). *The developing person through childhood* (6th ed.). New York, NY: Worth Publishing.

Bernier, A., Carlson, S. M., Deschênes, M., & Matte-Gagné, C. (2012). Social factors in the development of early executive functioning: A closer look at the caregiving environment. *Developmental Science, 15*, 12–24. doi:10.1111/j.1467-7687.2011.01093.x

Birmingham, R. S., Bub, K. L., & Vaughan, B. E. (2017). Parenting in infancy and self-regulation in preschool: An investigation of the role of attachment history. *Attachment and Human Behavior*, *19*(2), 107–129.

Bowlby, J. (1988). *A secure base: Parent-child attachment and healthy human development.* New York, NY: Basic Books.

Bradley, R. H., McKelvey, L. M., & Whiteside-Mansell, L. (2011). Does the quality of stimulation and support in the home environment moderate the effect of early education programs? *Child Development, 82*, 2110–2122. doi:10.1111/j.1467-8624.2011.01659.x

Campbell, F. A., Wasik, B. H., Pungello, E., Burchinal, M., Barbarin, O., Kainz, K., … Ramey, C. T. (2008). Young adult outcomes of the Abecedarian and CARE early childhood educational interventions. *Early Childhood Research Quarterly, 23*(4), 452–466.

Centers for Disease Control (CDC). (2018, June 19). *Learn the signs. Act early*. Retrieved from https://www.cdc.gov/ncbddd/actearly/milestones/index.html.

Chapman, G., & Campbell, R. (2005). *The five love languages of children.* Chicago, IL: Northfield Publishing.

Christiansen, S. L., & Stueve, J. L. (2004). Fathering with love and nurturance. In S. E. Brotherson & J. M. White (Eds.), *Why fathers count.* Harriman, TN: Men's Studies Press.

Clark, N. S., Hirsch, J. L., & Monin, J. K. (2019). Love conceptualized as mutual communal responsiveness. In R. J. Sternberg & K. Sternberg (Eds.), *The new psychology of love* (2nd ed). Cambridge, UK: Cambridge University Press.

Cousins, S. B. (2017). Practitioners' constructions of love in early childhood education and care. *International Journal of Early Years Education, 25*(10), 16–29.

Delahooke, M. (2017). *Social and emotional development in early intervention.* Eau Claire, WI: PESI Publishing.

Dempsey-Jones, H. (2017, March 23). *Touch in infancy is important for brain development*. Retrieved from https://theconversation.com/touch-in-infancy-is-important-for-healthy-brain-development-74864

Department of Education. (2004). Individuals with Disabilities Education Act (IDEA) Part C: Infants and toddlers with disabilities, Pub. L. No. 108-446 § 631. Findings and Policy.

Duffin, E. (2020, January 13). *Number of U.S. children living in a single parent family 1970–2019*. Retrieved from https://www.statista.com/statistics/252847/number-of-children-living-with-a-single-mother-or-single-father/

Duhig, A. M., Renk, K., Epstein, M. K., & Phares, V. (2000). Interparental agreement on internalizing, externalizing, and total behavior problems: A meta-analysis. *Clinical Psychology: Science and Practice, 7*, 435–453.

Eanes, R. (2016). *Positive parenting: An essential guide.* New York, NY: Penguin Random House.

Epstein, J. L. (2010). School/family/community partnerships: Caring for the children we share. *Phi Delta Kappan, 92*(3), 81–96.

Fay-Stammbach, T., Hawes, D. J., & Meredith, P. (2014). Parenting influences on executive function in early childhood: A review. *Child Development Perspectives, 8*, 258–264. doi:10.1111/cdep.12095

Fehr, B. (2019). Everyday conceptions of love. In R. J. Sternberg & K. Sternberg (Eds.), *The new psychology of love* (2nd ed.; pp. 154-182). Cambridge, UK: Cambridge University Press.

Fehr, B., & Russell, J. A. (1991). The concept of love viewed from a prototype perspective. *Journal of Personality and Social Psychology, 60,* 425–438.

Fink G., Peet E., Andrews K., McCoy, D. C., Sudfeld, C. R., Danaei, G., … Fawzi, W. W. (2015). Schooling and wage income losses due to early childhood developmental delays in low- and middle-income countries: National, regional and global estimates. *American Journal Clinical Nutrition, 104*, 104–112.

Fox, N. A., & Rutter, M. (2010). Introduction to the special section on the effects of early experience on development. *Child Development, 81*, 23–27.

Gardiner, K. E. (2003). Children's perception of parental love as a function of parental gender and gender of child. *Dissertation Abstracts International, 64/02* (AAT 3080403).

Galindo, C., & Sheldon, S. B. (2012). School and home connections and children's preschool achievement gains: The mediating role of family involvement. *Early Childhood Research Quarterly, 27*(1), 90–103.

Gerhardt, S. (2015). *Why love matters: How affection shapes in a baby's brain.* New York, NY: Routledge.

Gormley, W. T., Phillips, D., Adelstein, S., & Shaw, C. (2010). Head Start's comparative advantage: Myth or reality? *The Policy Studies Journal, 38*(3), 397–418.

Green, B. L., Everhart, M., Gordon, L., & Gettman, M. G. (2006). Characteristics of effective mental health consultation in early childhood settings: Multi-level analysis of a national survey. *Topics in Early Childhood Special Education, 26*(3), 142–152.

Green, B. L., Masch, A. M., Kothari, B. H., Busse, J., & Brennan, E. (2012). An intervention to increase early childhood staff capacity for promoting children's social-emotional development in preschool settings. *Early Childhood Education Journal, 40,* 123–132. doi:10.1007/s10643-011-0497-2

Griffin Technology. (2011, February 14). Retrieved from https://blog.griffintechnology.com/community/150-words-that-describe-love/

Guerra, N. G., Graham, S., & Tolan, P. H. (2011). Raising healthy children: Translating child development research into practice. *Childhood Development, 82*(1), 7–16.

Haider, S. K., & Ali, S. (2013). The significance of early childhood education in endorsing healthy child development. *PUTAJ—Humanities and Social Sciences, 20*, 137–145.

Heckman, J. J. (2006). Skill formation and the economics of investing in disadvantaged children. *Science, 312*, 1900–1902.

Heckman, J. J., Stixrud, J., & Urzua, S. (2006). The effects of cognitive and noncognitive abilities on labor market outcomes and social behavior. *Journal of Labor Economics, 24*(3), 411–482.

Horvath, C. A., Lee, C. M., & Bax, K. (2015). How similar are mothers and fathers of young children in their parenting responses and goals? *Journal of Child Family Studies, 24,* 3542–3551.

Hughes, C., & Ensor, R. (2009). How do families help or hinder the emergence of early executive function? *New Directions for Child and Adolescent Development, 123*, 35–50. doi:10.1002/cd.234

Johns, S. (2010). Early childhood service development and intersectoral collaboration in rural Australia. *Australian Journal of Primary Health, 16*, 40–46.

Johnson, L. J. (2007). *Parental love: As defined and expressed by parents of young children* (Doctoral dissertation). Available from ProQuest Dissertations and Theses database.

Kelly, K. R. (2015) Insecure attachment representations and child personal narrative structure: implications for delayed discourse in preschool-age children, *Attachment & Human Development, 17*(5), 448–471. doi:10.1080/14616734.2015.1076011

Knight, Z. G. (2017). A proposed model of psychodynamic psychotherapy linked to Erik Erikson's eight stages of psychosocial development. *Clinical Child Psychotherapy, 24*, 1047–1058.

Kramer, S. (2019, December 12). *U.S. has the single highest rate of children living in a single parent household.* Retrieved from https://www.pewresearch.org/fact-tank/2019/12/12/u-s-children-more-likely-than-children-in-other-countries-to-live-with-just-one-parent/

Lamb, M. E., & Lewis, C. (2011). The role of parent-child relationships in child development. In M. H. Bornstein & M. E. Lamb (Eds.), *Developmental science: An advanced textbook* (6th ed., pp. 469–517). New York, NY: Taylor and Francis.

Lewis, C., & Carpendale, J. I. M. (2009). Introduction: Links between social interaction and executive function. *New Directions for Child and Adolescent Development, 123*, 1–15. doi:10.1002/cd.232

Lickenbrock, D. M., Ekas, N.V., & Whitman, T. L. (2011). Feeling good, feeling bad: Influences of maternal perceptions of the child and marital adjustment on well-being in mothers of children with an autism spectrum disorder. *Journal of Autism Developmental Disorder, 41,* 848–858.

Lickona, T. (2008). *The power of modeling in children's character development.* In D. Steight (Ed.), *Parenting for character, five experts, five practices* (pp, 33-47). Portland, OR: Council for Spiritual and Ethical Education.

Lugo-Gil, J., & Tamis-LeMonda, C. S. (2008). Family resources and parenting quality: Links to children's cognitive development across the first 3 years. *Child Development, 79*, 1065–1085.

Matte-Gagné, C., & Bernier, A. (2011). Prospective relations between maternal autonomy support and child executive functioning: Investigating the mediating role of child language ability. *Journal of Experimental Child Psychology, 110*, 611–625. doi:10.1016/j.jecp.2011.06.006

McCartney, K., Dearing, E., Taylor, B. A., & Bub, K. L. (2007). Quality childcare supports achievement of low-income children: Direct and indirect pathways through caregiving and the home environment. *Applied Developmental Psychology, 28*, 411–426. doi:10.1016/j.appdev.2007.06.010

McCoy, D. C., Sudfeld, D. R., Bellinger, D. C., Muhihi, A., Ashery, G., Weary, T. E., … Fink, G. (2017). Development and validation of an early childhood development scale for use in low-resourced settings. *Population Health Metrics, 15*(3), 1–18.

Meeker, M. (2017, April 26). *The difference between moms and dads*. Retrieved from https://www.megmeekermd.com/blog/difference-between-moms-and-dads/

Merriam-Webster. (2019). Retrieved from https://www.merriam-webster.com/thesaurus/loving

Morris, A. S., Silk, J. S., Steinberg, L., Myers, S. S., & Robinson, R. (2007). The role of the family context in the development of emotion regulation. *Social Development, 16*(2), 361–388.

Newton, R. P. (2008). *The attachment connection: Parenting a secure and confident child using the science of attachment theory.* Oakland, CA: Harbinger Publications.

Nores, M., & Barnett, W. S. (2010). Benefits of early childhood interventions across the world: (Under) investing in the very young. *Economic Education Review, 29*, 271–282.

Norris, V., & Rodwell, H. (2017). *Parenting with theraplay.* Philadelphia, PA: Jessica Kingsley Publishers.

O'Connor, T. G. (2002). Annotation: The "effects" of parenting reconsidered: Findings, challenges, and applications. *Journal of Child Psychology and Psychiatry, 43*, 555–572. doi:10.1111/1469-7610.0046

O'Reilly, J. O., & Peterson, C. C. (2014). Theory of mind at home: Linking authoritative and authoritarian parenting styles to children's social understanding. *Early Child Development and Care, 184*(12), 1934–1947.

Palmer, V. (2016, August 5). The 13 key benefits of early childhood education: A teacher's perspective. *Huffington Post.* Retrieved from https://www.huffingtonpost.com/vicki-palmer/the-13-key-benefits-of-ea_b_7943348.html

Peet, E. D., McCoy D. C., Goodarz, Z. D., Ezzarti, M., Fawiz, W., Marjo-Riitta, J., … Fink, G. (2015). Early childhood development and schooling attainment:

Longitudinal evidence from British, Finnish and Philippine birth cohorts. *PLoS ONE, 10*(9), 1–20.

Ponzio, F. J., Jr., & Madonna, S. (2019a). *Parenting with love ideas.* [Pamphlet]. People Technology Foundation.

Ponzio, F. J., Jr., & Madonna, S. (2019b). *Teach your child love: With pre-K love and pre-K ed.* [Pamphlet]. [Kindle DX Version]. People Technology Foundation.

Raver, C. C., Jones, S. M., Li-Grining, C. P., Zhai, F., Metzger, M. W., & Solomon, B. (2009). Targeting children's behavior problems in preschool classrooms: A cluster-randomized controlled trial. *Journal of Consulting and Clinical Psychology, 77*, 302–316.

Rohner, R. P., & Veneziano, R. A. (2001). The importance of father love: History and contemporary evidence. *Review of General Psychology, 5*(4), 382–405.

Sanchez, L. (2015, July 14). The "Head Start" early childhood education gave me [Video file]. TEDx Talks. Retrieved from https://www.youtube.com/watch?v=dmSMQX68Fec

Sheridan, S. M., Knoche, L. L., Edwards, C. P., Bovaird, J. A., & Kupzyk, K. A. (2010). Parent engagement and school readiness: Effects of the Getting Ready Intervention on preschool children's social-emotional competencies. *Early Education and Development, 21*(1), 125–156.

Shonkoff, J. P. (2010). Building a new biodevelopmental framework to guide the future of early childhood policy. *Child Development, 81*, 357–367.

Shonkoff, J. P., & Levitt, P. (2010). Neuroscience and the future of early childhood policy: Moving from why to what and how. *Neuron, 67*(5), 689–691.

Sol, M. (2019). *39 self-care ideas for those who struggle with self-love.* Retrieved from https://lonerwolf.com/self-care-ideas/

Solheim, E., Wichstrøm, L., Belsky, J., & Berg-Neilson, T. S. (2013). Do time in childcare and peer group exposure predict poor socioemotional adjustment in Norway? *Child Development, 84*(5), 1701–1715.

Sroufe, A. (2005). Attachment and development: A prospective, longitudinal study from birth to adulthood. *Attachment and Human Development, 7*(4), 349–367.

Streight, D. (Ed.). (2008). *Parenting for character, five experts, five practices.* Portland, OR: Council for Spiritual and Ethical Education.

The Holy Bible, New International Version. (1984). Grand Rapids: Zondervan Publishing House.

Thesaurus.com. (2019). Loving. Retrieved from https://www.thesaurus.com/browse/loving

Thomas, R. M. (1996). *Comparing theories of child development*. Pacific Grove, CA: Brooks/Cole Publishing.

U.S. Department of Health and Human Services (USDHHS). (2010, January). *Head Start impact study.* Final Report. Retrieved from https://www.acf.hhs.gov/opre/resource/head-start-impact-study-final-report-executive-summary

Wachs, T. D. (2000). *Necessary but not sufficient.* Washington, DC: American Psychological Association.

Wass, S. V. (2015). Applying cognitive training to target executive functions during early development. *Child Neuropsychology, 21*(2), 150–166.

Watson, M. (2008). *Discipline strategies that support character growth.* In D. Steight (Ed.), *Parenting for character, five experts, five practices* (pp. 51–63).

Yerkovich, M., & Yerokvich, K. (2011). *How we love our kids: The five love styles of parenting.* Colorado Springs, CO: Waterbrook Press.

Zelina, G. (2017). *The loving dad's handbook.* Columbia, SC: Author.

Zhang, Q. (2015). Defining "meaningfulness": Enabling preschoolers to get the most out of parental involvement. *Australasian Journal of Early Childhood, 40*(4), 212–220.

Appendix A

About the People Technology Foundation

The PTF was formed in 1993 as a 501(c)(3) nonprofit organization, which means that donations to the Foundation are tax deductible. Its EIN is 22-3273424. If you are interested in contributing to our efforts, we appreciate any financial donations, donations in-kind, and donation of your efforts.

Frank J. Ponzio Jr. is founder and CEO of the PTF and has a rich history of philanthropic endeavors in the United States and Romania. For more information, see the PTF web site below.

Contact Information

Please contact the authors at
info@peopletechnologyfoundation.org
The web site is: www.peopletechnologyfoundation.org

PTF Publications
The PTF has published *Military Systems Information Quality* (Amazon.com; search keywords “Ponzio Quality”)

Nov. 20, 2017

Three versions of *Two Notre Dame Alumni* (Amazon.com; search keywords “Ponzio Alumni”)

with grey-scale photos

with enhanced color photos

Kindle version

Pamphlets entitled *Parenting With Love Ideas* and *Teach Your Child Love*.
(Amazon.com; search keywords "Ponzio Love")

August 17, 2019

November 9, 2019

January 9, 2020

We have recently published a Kindle version of *Pre-K Attachment and Parental Love*
(Amazon.com; search keywords "Ponzio Love")

May 19, 2020

About the Authors

Frank J. Ponzio Jr. was born in the United States to immigrant parents who did not finish elementary school. He attended public schools and graduated from a prep school in New Jersey and was accepted into the University of Notre Dame in South Bend, Indiana.

He received a bachelor's degree in Engineering from Notre Dame in 1959. Notre Dame then awarded him a fellowship for his master's degree in Engineering, which he received in 1961. He later received a master's degree in Technology Management from Stevens Institute of Technology in Hoboken, New Jersey.

He was employed in industry in the areas of Ballistic Missile Guidance Systems and International Communications computer systems.

In 1968 he started his own company, Symbolic Systems, to develop and sell business applications for minicomputers. The company then expanded into the services business, providing services on military bases to prepare weapon systems computer deployment into a Warfare Theater of Operations. Symbolic Systems also expanded the use of Social Media Technologies in Department of Defense operations.

In 2015, after 47 years in business, he sold the assets of Symbolic Systems and retired.

While in retirement, Frank is actively involved in authoring books on a variety of subjects for the People Technology Foundation, the titles of which are listed in the previous section of this book.

The first book is about military weapon systems data. The second is about People Technology Foundation's humanitarian efforts in Romania, a former Iron Curtain country.

The current book is based on efforts and objectives listed in two pamphlets listed in the previous section of this book (*Teach Your Child Love* and *Parenting With Love Ideas*).

Dr. Stephen Madonna was born and raised in New Jersey, where he graduated from high school. He attended the University of Tampa, where he received a BA in Psychology and went on to earn an MA and PhD in Psychology from the University of Southern Mississippi. After teaching and working in the field of psychology for a number of years, he went back to school, first to complete a master's degree in Public Administration (MPA) from Troy University, and later a master's degree in Instructional Leadership (MEd) from Saint Leo University.

Currently, Dr. Madonna is a part-time Professor of Psychology at the University of Maryland, Global Campus as well as Adjunct Faculty at Saint Leo University. He has taught psychology and education at several colleges and universities over the past 32 years, including: Hillsborough Community College, Excelsior College, Troy University, and William Carey College. He has taught on military bases, both overseas (Japan, Korea, and the Philippines) and in the U.S. (Mississippi and Florida). He has taught on traditional college campuses, satellite facilities, and online. He also spent 11 years working in the field of intellectual and developmental disabilities as a psychologist, administrator, and behavior analyst.

Dr. Madonna's research interests include Collaborative Leadership models, data-based decision making, online learning strategies and the adult learner, as well as situational and dispositional characteristics of the adult learner. He has published 21 papers and has presented at state, regional, and national meetings.

Made in the USA
Middletown, DE
06 June 2021

40458674R00073